WHAT'S NEXT FOR THE UN?
UNDERSTANDING GLOBAL ISSUES

Published by Smart Apple Media
1980 Lookout Drive
North Mankato, Minnesota 56003
USA

This book is based on *What Next for the UN? The Challenges of Global Disorder*,
Copyright ©1999 Understanding Global Issues Ltd., Cheltenham, England.

Library of Congress Cataloging-in-Publication Data

What next for the UN? / edited by Michael Lowry.
    p. cm. -- (Understanding global issues)
Includes index.
Summary: Examines the history and work of the United Nations, including
its efforts against such problems as poverty, human rights violations,
and terrorism.
  ISBN 1-58340-167-9 (hardcover : alk. paper)
  1. United Nations--Juvenile literature. [1. United Nations.] I.
Lowry, Mike, 1919- II. Series.
  JZ4984.6 .W475 2002
  341.23--dc21

                              2001008446

                    Printed in Malaysia
                    2 4 6 8 9 7 5 3 1

EDITOR Michael Lowry   **COPY EDITOR** Jennifer Nault
PHOTO RESEARCHER Gayle Murdoff   **DESIGNER** Terry Paulhus

Contents

Introduction

The 21st century has begun with a new kind of battle—a war against terrorism. On Tuesday, September 11, 2001, terrorists attacked the United States. The attacks, which caused more than 3,000 deaths, horrified people all around the world. The resulting war on terrorism received the support of most member countries of the United Nations (UN)—the organization set up to enable countries to work together for peace and mutual development.

The threat of terrorism has had a profound effect on the global community. Many governments have passed controversial new laws to help combat terrorism, while law enforcement agencies around the world cooperate with one another to arrest suspected terrorists. Relationships between the countries of the world are being redefined. The president of the United States, George W. Bush, has placed countries into two categories: those against terrorism and those who support or harbor terrorists. While this separation is intended

The flags of all 189 United Nations member countries fly along First Avenue in front of the UN headquarters in New York. The flags are placed in alphabetical order.

to simplify the current world situation, the reality is much more complex.

When countries join the UN, they agree to follow its Charter. The UN Charter is a statement of principles that promotes peace, human rights, and friendship between countries. If all member states were to abide by the

> *The UN Charter is a statement of principles that promote peace, human rights, and friendship between countries.*

Charter, the world would be a much better place, with peace and harmony, equal rights, social progress, and higher standards of living. In fact, there is a wide gap between **rhetoric** and reality, and terrorism is only the latest item on a growing list of world problems. Civil wars, ethnic cleansing, and widespread abuses of human rights continue today despite 50 years of UN efforts.

It is the task of the Security Council, which is a branch of the UN, to maintain international peace and security. During the Cold War, there was very little cooperation among members of the Security Council, who were often at odds with each other. As a result, the Security Council was unable to enforce the UN's resolutions. This reflected poorly on the UN's reputation as international peacekeeper. Reform of the Security Council would help legitimize the UN, which is still seen by many to be dominated by the United States.

During the past 10 years, the UN has changed the way it operates. To become more efficient, the UN has cut staff, closed down departments, reduced budgets, and introduced new management practices. But funding is still the biggest problem for the UN, as many countries do not pay their membership **dues**. The United States, which was responsible for paying one-quarter of UN costs, did not pay its dues for many years. Consequently, there was a period when the UN had almost no money at all.

Despite financial problems and internal rivalries, the UN is a powerful force for change. In addition to international peacekeeping missions, the UN has launched a campaign to stop the use of land mines. The UN has also helped to create the new International Criminal Court. In this court, presumed terrorists and dictators can be tried for committing crimes against humanity.

The Founding of the UN

In 1918, at the end of World War I, the nations that won the war came together to form the League of Nations. Their intent was to create an international organization that promoted cooperation, peace, and security between countries of the world. The United States did not join, in part because Article X of the Covenant of the League of Nations required members to unite together against any future aggression. At the time, many Americans opposed U.S. involvement in world affairs. Without the United States, the League was not as

With the end of World War II, the world rejoiced. This sense of optimism was reflected in the language of the UN Charter.

strong as it could have been. However, the League did succeed in establishing the International Labour Organization (ILO), the High Commissioner for Refugees, the International Court of Justice, and various other bodies, some of which were later adopted by the UN.

During the 1930s, Germany and Japan began invading other countries. The League of Nations could not agree on how to deal with this new aggression. When World War II began in 1939, the League collapsed in disarray.

During World War II, 26 countries agreed to come together to form the UN. In 1944, China, the Soviet Union, the United Kingdom, and the United States agreed on the basic idea of the UN Charter. The Charter was written at a convention in San Francisco in 1945. The UN came into official existence on October 24, 1945. The name of the United Nations was coined by the United States President Franklin D. Roosevelt. There were 50 countries that signed the UN Charter that day. In honor of the occasion, October 24th has been named UN Day.

With the end of World War II, the world rejoiced. This sense

A converted ice-skating rink in Flushing Meadows Park, New York, served as the temporary headquarters of the United Nations between 1946 and 1949.

of optimism was reflected in the language of the UN Charter. Soon, however, the Cold War began. During the Cold War, the United States and the Soviet Union engaged in an **arms race** and became very suspicious of one another. The two countries had very different ideas about how to govern. Since both countries were members of the Security Council, there was little progress in furthering international peace. With the inaction of the Security Council, the UN began to devote its energies to other areas of global concern.

Over the years, more countries joined the UN. By 1960, there were 100 member countries in the organization. By 1970, there were 127 countries. And by 1980, 154 countries had joined the UN. Today, there are 189 countries that belong to the UN. As more **developing countries** joined the UN, its interests began to reflect those

▨ **The UN High Commissioner for Refugees (UNHCR) provides humanitarian relief to more than 22 million refugees worldwide.**

of the Third World. In the 1980s, disagreement within the Security Council and the UN's increasing

THE FIRST CHALLENGE OF THE UN

The UN's first major crisis occurred soon after it was formed. In 1948, the creation of the Jewish state of Israel resulted in a war between the Arabs and the Israelis in the Middle East. Count Folke Bernadotte, who had been sent by the UN to negotiate a settlement, was assassinated by Jewish terrorists on September 17, 1948. Ultimately, the UN failed to resolve the situation. The conflict between Israel and surrounding Arab nations continues to this day. Located in Jerusalem, the UN Truce Supervision Organization has been monitoring the region since 1948.

involvement in the Third World resulted in a lack of support for UN activities among the world's richer countries, including the United States.

The end of the Cold War, however, breathed new life into the UN. In January 1992, Egypt's former foreign minister, Dr. Boutros Boutros-Ghali, became the UN's new Secretary-General. He was determined to revitalize the organization and make it a more powerful force, both for peacekeeping and for economic and social development throughout the world. Although his methods were sometimes controversial, all Security Council members except the U.S. voted for his reappointment in 1996.

UN MEMBER COUNTRIES

Today, almost every country in the world is a member of the UN. Until recently, the most notable exception was Switzerland. The Swiss people voted to join the UN in March of 2002. Switzerland has long been a member of various UN agencies. The city of Geneva in Switzerland is an important center for UN activities. The headquarters of the World Health Organization (WHO), the Office of the UN High Commissioner for Refugees (UNHCR), and the Economic Commission for Europe (ECE) are all in Geneva. Vatican City, Nauru, and Tonga also contribute to the UN, even though they are not members. The only other non-members of the UN in 2002 were Taiwan and a few small island states.

However, without the support of the United States, Boutros-Ghali lost the post and the position went to the diplomatic Kofi Annan from Ghana. Annan, who knew the UN inside out, shared Boutros Ghali's passion for reform but showed a more flexible style of management. Annan was appointed to serve a second term beginning January 2002.

KEY CONCEPTS

League of Nations The League of Nations was established as an alliance dedicated to maintaining world peace. Twenty-eight countries remained permanent members throughout its existence, with another 35 countries holding memberships at one time or another. While the League experienced limited success, it ultimately ceased operations at the beginning of World War II. It was replaced by the UN in 1946.

The Cold War Journalist Walter Lippman first used the term "Cold War" to refer to the tensions that had developed between the United States and the former Soviet Union after the end of World War II. The Cold War resulted in two military alliances: the North Atlantic Treaty Organization (NATO), which represented the United States and its allies; and the Warsaw Pact, which represented the Soviet Union and its allies. While the United States and the Soviet Union never engaged in direct confrontation, many conflicts around the globe were linked to Cold War hostilities. The two countries did engage in an arms race, which saw a dramatic increase in the number of nuclear and other weapons produced in both countries. The Cold War ended around 1989, following

the decline of Soviet power in Eastern Europe, and the symbolic destruction of the Berlin Wall.

UN Charter The UN Charter was signed on June 26, 1945, in San Francisco and came into effect on October 24, 1945. The Charter outlines the purposes of the UN: to maintain international peace and security; to develop friendly relations among states; and to achieve cooperation in solving international economic, social, cultural, and humanitarian problems. The document is made up of a preamble and 19 chapters, which are divided into 111 articles.

PART OF THE PREAMBLE TO THE UN CHARTER

Drafted by South African military leader and statesman Jan Christiaan Smuts in 1945, the preamble to the UN Charter sets a positive precedent for the entire document. The charter was considered so valuable that when it was flown to Washington, D.C., it was attached to a parachute.

"We, the peoples of the United Nations, determined to save succeeding generations from the scourge of war, which twice in our lifetime has brought untold sorrow to mankind, and to reaffirm faith in fundamental human rights, in the dignity and worth of the human person, in the equal rights of men and women and of nations large and small, and to establish conditions under which justice and respect for the obligations arising from treaties and other sources of international law can be maintained, and to promote social progress and better standards of life in larger freedom, and for these ends to practice tolerance and live together in peace with one another as good neighbours, and to unite our strength to maintain international peace and security, and to ensure, by the acceptance of principles and the institution of methods, that armed force shall not be used, save in the common interest, and to employ international machinery for the promotion of the economic and social advancement of all peoples, have resolved to combine our efforts to accomplish these aims."

The UN Charter emphasizes the need to protect the human rights of all men, women, and children, regardless of race or religion.

A Parliament of Nations

The General Assembly sets the agenda for UN operations. It is the closest thing there is to a world parliament, but it has no law-making powers. When the countries of the UN meet as a group, they are called the General Assembly. When the General Assembly meets, each country, rich or poor, large or small, has the chance to speak up and be heard on any matter. Every country may have up to five representatives, but is entitled to only one vote, no matter what its size or population. Important questions are decided by a two-thirds majority. Procedural questions require a simple majority, which means more than half. Since the decisions made by the General Assembly do not have the power of law, countries are not forced to abide by them. However, the pressure of the world's opinion carries tremendous weight.

The General Assembly typically meets between September and December each year. In recent years, the Assembly has been in session throughout the entire year. Other groups in the UN meet and work throughout the year. The General Assembly may also meet for special sessions to discuss specific topics of global concern, such as the June 2001 meeting on the global AIDS epidemic.

> **When the General Assembly meets, each country, rich or poor, large or small, has the chance to speak.**

Emergency special sessions can be called within 24 hours, if requested by the Security Council. The General Assembly elects a new president at the beginning of each yearly session. The president is responsible for directing the discussions of the Assembly.

The topics discussed by the General Assembly must fall within the scope of the UN Charter. The decisions of the General Assembly guide the UN's actions and activities. The General Assembly also discusses how much money the UN will spend and in what ways it will spend it. The Assembly is responsible for appointing the non-permanent members of the Security Council.

While the General Assembly may discuss issues related to international peace and security, including disarmament and the regulation of arms, only the Security Council can take action on specific security disputes. Article 24 of the UN Charter states that specific security problems may only be addressed by the Security Council. Often, the decisions made by the General Assembly

The General Assembly Hall can seat more than 1,800 people and is the largest room at the UN headquarters in New York. The hall is the only conference room at the UN that contains the UN emblem.

THE SIX COMMITTEES OF THE GENERAL ASSEMBLY

The General Assembly discusses a wide range of topics. Discussion of these topics is assigned to one of six main committees:

1. The Disarmament and International Security Committee
2. The Economic and Financial Committee
3. The Social, Humanitarian, and Cultural Committee
4. The Special Political and Decolonization Committee
5. The Administrative and Budgetary Committee
6. The Legal Committee

are very different from the actions taken by the Security Council.

Membership in the UN is open to all peace-loving countries that accept the UN Charter. Despite this, there are many countries in the General Assembly whose values are not in agreement with the Charter. Some countries are ruled by tyrants—leaders who treat their people with cruelty and who hold power without any legal right to do so.

The UN Charter allows the General Assembly to expel any country that violates the principles of the Charter, but this has never happened. South Africa, Israel, and Iraq are all countries that have come into conflict with the UN. While the General Assembly has been very critical of the behavior of these countries, they have not expelled them.

Serbia and Montenegro, which were part of the former Yugoslavia, have also come under criticism. In 1992, the UN decided that Serbia and Montenegro were not allowed to be part of the General Assembly based on Yugoslavia's membership. According to the UN, Serbia and Montenegro had to reapply to become members of the UN. In 1992, Serbia and Montenegro joined together to form the Federal Republic of Yugoslavia, which was admitted as a member of the UN in November 2000. That is the closest any country has come to being expelled from the UN.

More than half of the 189 countries that belong to the UN have freely elected governments. Thirty other countries may soon have free elections. The worldwide trend is toward greater democracy and the opening of trade barriers.

KEY CONCEPTS

Democracy Democracy is a form of government that is ruled by the people. Democracy can either be direct or representative. Ancient Athens was a direct democracy, where the people were able to gather to vote on laws and other issues. Today, most democratic societies elect representatives to form a government that governs on behalf of the people. The majority of democratic societies value freedom and equality for their citizens. Three of the key freedoms of democracy are freedom of speech, freedom of the press, and freedom of religion.

Tyranny Tyranny is a form of government whereby a single ruler claims absolute power. Tyrannical rule is often characterized by cruelty and the **suppression** of freedom. Tyrannical rulers, or tyrants, typically resort to force as a means of maintaining order within society.

Decolonization Decolonization refers to the process by which a colonized territory gains independence. In 1945, when the United Nations was formed, about 750 million people still lived in colonized territories. Today, that number has fallen to less than two million people. Since 1945, more than 80 former colonies have joined the United Nations as independent countries.

Duties: Help run the operations of the UN

Education: A university degree in a related field, such as economics or political science

Interests: Politics, economics, and the welfare of society

Navigate to the UN's Office of Human Resources Management Web site: www.un.org/Depts/OHRM/index.html for information on related careers. Also click on www.opm.gov for more information on employment with the federal government of the United States.

Careers in Focus

International civil servants are the body of officials and clerks who are responsible for the day-to-day administrative work of the various departments of the UN. Virtually every staff position within the UN fits this description. UN positions include administrator, economist, electronic data processor, accountant, lawyer, librarian, political advisor, public relations officer, social development officer, and statistician.

All international civil servant positions within the UN require a university degree in a field related to the area of interest. Fluency in more than one language is preferred. English and French are the working languages of the UN. During their careers, UN staff are expected to serve at various duty stations throughout the world. Therefore, a willingness to relocate and to live in another country is important.

The requirements for UN positions vary. To qualify for an entry-level position, an applicant must possess a first-level university degree and be 32 years of age or younger. For a mid-level position, an applicant must possess an advanced university degree, four years of related professional experience, and be 39 years of age or younger. Applicants must also believe in the goals and ideals of the UN.

Specialized agencies of the UN, such as the Food and Agriculture Organization (FAO), conduct their own recruitment programs.

The Security Council

According to Article 24 of the UN Charter, the Security Council is responsible for maintaining peace in the world. Fifteen countries are members of the Security Council. Five of those countries are permanent members: the People's Republic of China, France, the Russian Federation, the United Kingdom, and the United States. The other 10 members are elected for 2-year terms by the General Assembly. Each member of the Security Council has one vote. Decisions on procedural matters can be passed if at least 9 of the 15 members agree. Decisions on important matters require the agreement of all five of the permanent members.

During the Cold War, the permanent members of the Security Council almost never agreed with each other.

During the Cold War, it was very difficult for all five of the permanent members of the Security Council to agree. In fact, it almost never happened, and the UN's ability to promote peace in the world was severely weakened. After the Cold War ended around 1989, members of the Security Council began to agree again. Recently, however, political differences have begun to resurface, mainly between western countries, such as the United States and the United Kingdom, and China and Russia.

The Security Council has a great deal of power. It can investigate any disagreement that might lead to war. It can suggest solutions. It can ask other countries to take action,

WAR AND PEACE

The world spends $800 billion a year on weapons but only a few billion dollars a year on peace. The 5 permanent members of the Security Council sell 85 percent of all the weapons worldwide. Between 1993 and 1999, the United States exported $184 billion in arms, the United Kingdom exported $59.5 billion, France exported $41.8 billion, and Russia exported $22 billion.

Military Spending of Selected UN Member Countries in 1999 (billions of dollars)

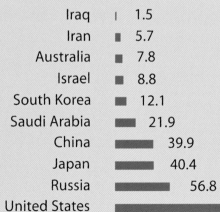

Iraq	1.5
Iran	5.7
Australia	7.8
Israel	8.8
South Korea	12.1
Saudi Arabia	21.9
China	39.9
Japan	40.4
Russia	56.8
United States	283.1

such as imposing economic sanctions. Finally, it can use military power to maintain peace and security.

According to the UN Charter, the Security Council is required to have an international army available for use at all times. However, disagreement among the permanent members of the Security Council has meant that a UN army was never created. This lack of military power has severely limited the UN's ability to enforce its resolutions.

When the UN was created in 1945, the five leading powers that had won the war against Germany and Japan established themselves as the five permanent members of the Security Council. They gave themselves the power to vote against any idea that they did not agree with. This power is called a veto. With a veto, each permanent member is able to ensure that their country's interests are protected. At first, there were only 6 non-permanent members, but the number was increased to 10 in 1966.

The world in the 21st century is very different from the world of the 1940s. The Security Council no longer reflects

The Security Council Chamber, known as the Norwegian Room, was a gift from Norway.

the realities of world politics. New major powers are emerging, such as Japan and Germany, which have the second- and third-largest economies in the

MEMBERS OF THE SECURITY COUNCIL

2002	Bulgaria, Cameroon, **People's Republic of China**, Colombia, **France**, Guinea, Ireland, Mauritius, Mexico, Norway, **Russian Federation**, Singapore, Syria, **United Kingdom**, **United States**
2001	Bangladesh, **People's Republic of China**, Colombia, **France**, Ireland, Jamaica, Mali, Mauritius, Norway, **Russian Federation**, Singapore, Tunisia, Ukraine, **United Kingdom**, **United States**

Note: Countries shown in bold are permanent members. Membership for non-permanent members lasts for two calendar years. A non-permanent member cannot serve two successive terms, but can be re-elected after an interval of one year.

world. Only the United States has a larger economy. Despite their economic strength, Germany and Japan are not permanent members of the Security Council. Instead, they must take their turn on the Council, just like much smaller countries, such as Cape Verde.

Other countries are also upset that they are not permanent members of the Security Council. India, Brazil, and Nigeria are important developing countries that think they should have a greater say in the Security Council. One suggestion is that members should be chosen from different regions of the world. Any change in the structure of the Security Council would require an agreement by the five permanent members to give up some of their power. This is unlikely to happen in the near future. Part of the reason the Security Council works is because it is fairly small. The question is how to create a new Security Council that is still effective, but gives developing countries a greater voice.

REFORM OF THE SECURITY COUNCIL

Reform of the Security Council is long overdue. The developing world argues that the Security Council is unfairly slanted toward the interests of the industrialized countries. Few would argue against the permanent membership of the "big three"—China, Russia, and the U.S.—and France and the United Kingdom both have much to offer in terms of international experience. Germany and Japan are two of the biggest contributors to the UN. These countries complain that they should be represented as permanent members since they contribute significantly more money. Some think that Europe should be represented on the Security Council by one European country. Many wonder whether the veto should be eliminated or changed.

In 1993, the General Assembly considered making changes to the Security Council. Many suggestions have been put forward. Many agree that the Security Council should be changed and that it should probably have more members, but no one knows how to do it. A change would require the support of two-thirds of the General Assembly and the agreement of the permanent five (P5).

Perhaps the Security Council could have 24 members, with 5 new permanent members—Germany, Japan, an African nation, an Asian nation, and a Latin-American nation—and 4 new non-permanent members from the developing world and Eastern Europe. This would create a Security Council that better reflects the global community. Decisions would require 15 votes. The original P5 could not be forced to give it up, but perhaps the veto could only be used in decisions involving the use of military force. Alternately, the veto could work only if at least one other permanent member used the veto at the same time. These are just some of the ideas under consideration.

Getting all five permanent members of the Security Council to agree to reduce their power would be difficult, though not impossible. Much would depend on the United States, where most of the UN's money comes from. As the only global superpower, the United States is the UN's unofficial "leader." The United States does not want a 24-member Council, on the grounds that it would be too big. According to the United States, 21 should be the largest number of members. It is clear that changes to the Security Council will not happen any time soon, unless there is a change in policy in the U.S.

The five permanent members of the UN Security Council were also the first five countries in the world to develop nuclear weapons.

KEY CONCEPTS

Economic Sanctions
Economic sanctions are limits on international trade that are placed upon a specific country as a form of persuasion or punishment. Sanctions can severely damage a country's economy. Today, there is much controversy surrounding the use of sanctions. While some people consider sanctions to be a means of solving conflict without the use of military force, others claim that sanctions are more damaging to a country's citizens than to the leaders they are supposed to punish. Between 1991 and 1996, economic sanctions placed upon Iraq are estimated to have resulted in the deaths of more than 500,000 children from starvation and a lack of medical care.

Veto A veto is a vote that has the power to block a decision made by others. Typically, any party or person that is given the power of veto will use it to reject a resolution with which they do not agree. In the UN, the five permanent members of the Security Council are given the power of veto.

The Complex UN System

The UN family of organizations, also known as the UN system, is a complex web of agencies, programs, and funds. The main activities are carried out by various **commissions** and committees, such as the Commission on Human Rights. There are also organs such as the UN High Commissioner for Refugees (UNHCR) and the United Nations Children's Fund (UNICEF), specialized agencies such as the International Labour Organization (ILO) and the Food and Agriculture Organization (FAO), and programs such as the United Nations Development Programme (UNDP) and the United Nations Environment Programme (UNEP). The International Atomic Energy Association (IAEA) is associated with the UN, but remains independent. The World Trade Organization is not part of the UN system but interacts with it.

The UN system is a network of institutions with overlapping responsibilities. The system was deliberately designed to keep power away from the center. It is very difficult to change the structure of the UN because power is spread out among so many different agencies and groups.

The UN Charter created six principal organs—the General Assembly, the Security Council, the International Court of Justice, the Economic and Social Council (ECOSOC), the Trusteeship Council, and the Secretariat. There are 54 members of the ECOSOC.

They coordinate programs that provide money and humanitarian aid to people around the world. The Trusteeship Council was set up to help with the decolonization process. The Council suspended its operations in 1994, when the last trust territory, Palau, gained independence from the United States and joined the UN as the 185th member.

One out of every 275 people on Earth is currently a refugee. Nearly 60 percent of these refugees are children.

THE COST OF PEACE

The cost of peacekeeping is shared by all UN member countries. The cost varies from year to year depending upon the operations. In 2000, peacekeeping operations cost $2.6 billion, or 30¢ for every person on Earth.

Leading Contributors to the Peacekeeping Operations Budget (1999)

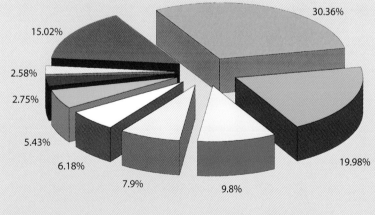

- 30.36%
- 15.02%
- 2.58%
- 2.75%
- 5.43%
- 6.18%
- 7.9%
- 9.8%
- 19.98%

☐ U.S.*   ☐ France   ■ Canada
☐ Japan   ☐ UK   ☐ Spain
☐ Germany   ☐ Italy   ■ Other Countries

*The U.S. contribution to the peacekeeping budget is expected to decline to 25 percent by 2004.

The Secretariat manages the UN. The head of the Secretariat is the Secretary-General. His or her staff carries out the day-to-day operations of the UN. The staff is comprised of international civil servants from around the world. More than 50,000 people work for the UN, but only 8,700 work in the Secretariat. As employees of the UN, they are expected to take their orders from the Secretary-General and not from their own governments. For the UN to work, its employees must be free to do things that their own governments may not like. They must also be able to work together with people from other countries. At times, disagreements between countries can interfere with the work of UN employees.

The UN is often accused of wasting time and money. Over the last decade, great efforts have been made to streamline the organization, but the UN is extremely resistant to change, and **reforms** have been slow to come. Even when reforms are initiated, they do not always affect the entire UN system.

Considering the vast responsibilities of the UN, its budget is extremely small. The UN's budget for its core activities is $1.25 billion per year, which is about 4 percent of New York City's annual budget. The U.S. share of the UN's budget for 1999 was $298 million, or $1.11 per American. By comparison, a small country such as San Marino pays $4.26 per citizen to the UN. The annual peacekeeping budget is even less, at $1 billion per year.

The cost to operate the entire UN system is about $12.5 billion per year, which is less than the operating costs of a large multinational business. There are about 52,000 people working for the UN worldwide. Companies such as Hitachi, Volkswagen, and McDonald's employ about three times that number of people.

UN SECRETARIES-GENERAL

The Secretary-General is recommended by the Security Council. The General Assembly then votes on the Secretary-General. The Secretary-General is appointed for five years and may be re-appointed at the end of his or her term.

In 1998, a new position was created to help manage the operations of the Secretariat. Louise Fréchette from Canada became the first Deputy Secretary-General.

Trygve Lie (Norway)	1946–1952
Dag Hammarskjöld (Sweden)	1953–1961
U Thant (Burma)	1961–1971
Kurt Waldheim (Austria)	1972–1981
Javier Pérez de Cuéllar (Peru)	1982–1991
Boutros Boutros-Ghali (Egypt)	1992–1996
Kofi Annan (Ghana)	1997–

KEY CONCEPTS

Peacekeeping Peacekeeping is a form of military action whereby special forces are sent to a region to preserve the peace. The presence of peacekeeping forces is intended to prevent previously warring sides from starting to fight again. The troops for these missions are drawn from the armed forces of UN member nations. Some of the many duties of peacekeeping forces include acting as buffers between warring forces, destroying surrendered weapons, monitoring **cease-fires**, and providing humanitarian aid.

Humanitarian Aid Humanitarian aid is emergency and long-term assistance given to countries in need of disaster relief. Disasters can be either natural, such as floods, or caused by human conflict, such as civil wars. Humanitarian aid comes in a variety of forms, including food, medicine, and temporary shelter.

SECURITY COUNCIL
(15 members)

Peacekeeping operations

Military Staff Committee

Standing committees and ad hoc bodies

ICTY
International Criminal Tribunal for the former Yugoslavia

ICTR
International Criminal Tribunal for Rwanda

UNSCOM
UN Special Commission (Iraq)

GENERAL ASSEMBLY
(all member states)

Main and other sessional committees

Standing committees and ad hoc bodies

Other subsidiary organs and related bodies

UNRWA
UN Relief & Works Agency for Palestine Refugees in the Near East

IAEA
International Atomic Energy Agency

WFP (UN / FAO)
World Food Programme

ITC
International Trade Centre (UNCTAD / WTO)

ECONOMIC & SOCIAL COUNCIL
(54 members)

Functional Commissions
* Social Development
* Crime Prevention & Criminal Justice
* Human Rights
* Narcotic Drugs
* Science & Technology for Development
* Sustainable Development
* Status of Women
* Population & Development
* Statistics

Regional Commissions
* Economic Commission for Africa (ECA)
* Economic Commission for Europe (ECE)
* Economic Commission for Latin America & the Caribbean (ECLAC)
* Economic and Social Committee for Asia & the Pacific (ESCAP)
* Economic & Social Committee for Western Asia (ESCWA)

Sessional and standing committees

Expert, ad hoc, and related bodies

SECRETARIAT
(8,700 staff)

Key offices of the Secretariat deal with administration (OSG), legal affairs (OLA), political affairs (DPA), disarmament (DDA), peacekeeping (DPKO), humanitarian affairs (OCHA), economic and social affairs (DESA) and public information (DPI).

INTERNATIONAL COURT OF JUSTICE
(15 judges)

INTERNATIONAL CRIMINAL COURT
(awaiting ratification)

TRUSTEESHIP COUNCIL
(activities suspended 1994)

Key

	Charter organs
	Other UN organs
	Other commissions, committees and ad hoc and related bodies
	UN programmes
	Specialized agencies & other autonomous organizations
	Independent body with special UN cooperation arrangements

UNDP
United Nations Development Programme

INSTRAW
International Research & Training Institute for the Advancement of Women

ODCCP
Office for Drug Control & Crime Prevention

OHCR
Office of the High Commissioner for Human Rights

UNCHS
United Nations Centre for Human Settlements (HABITAT)

UNCTAD
United Nations Conference on Trade & Development

UNIFEM
UN Development Fund for Women

UNV
United Nations Volunteers

UNEP
United Nations Environment Programme

UNFPA
United Nations Population Fund

UNHCR
Office of the UN High Commissioner for Refugees

UNICEF
United Nations Children's Fund

UNICRI
UN Interregional Crime & Justice Research Institute

UNIDIR
UN Institute for Disarmament Research

UNITAR
United Nations Institute for Training & Research

UNOPS
UN Office for Project Services

UNU
United Nations University

ILO
International Labour Organization

FAO
Food and Agriculture Organization

UNESCO
UN Educational, Scientific, and Cultural Organization

WHO
World Health Organization

World Bank group
IBRD
International Bank for Reconstruction and Development
IDA
International Development Association
IFC
International Finance Corporation
MIGA
Multilateral Investment Guarantee Agency

WTO
World Trade Organization

IMF
International Monetary Fund

ICAO
International Civil Aviation Organization

UPU
Universal Postal Union

ITU
International Telecommunication Union

WMO
World Meteorological Organization

IMO
International Maritime Organization

WIPO
World Intellectual Property Organization

IFAD
International Fund for Agricultural Development

UNIDO
United Nations Industrial Development Organization

THE UNITED NATIONS CHILDREN'S FUND

The United Nations Children's Fund (UNICEF) was established by the United Nations in 1946 to help children throughout the world. UNICEF is funded entirely by the voluntary contributions of governments and individuals. In 1989, UNICEF adopted the Convention on the Rights of the Child, which outlined the basic human rights for children everywhere. The Convention is the most widely accepted human rights treaty ever, and it has been **ratified** by 191 countries. Each country that ratifies the Convention is responsible for ensuring that the rights of children are protected within their country. The Convention is guided by four main principles:

- Children must not suffer discrimination "irrespective of the child's or his or her parent's or legal guardian's race, color, sex, language, religion, political or other opinion, national, ethnic or social origin, property, disability, birth or other status."

- Children have a right to survival and development in all aspects of their lives, including the physical, emotional, psycho-social, **cognitive**, social and cultural.

- The best interests of the child must be a primary consideration in all decisions or actions that affect the child or children as a group. This holds true whether decisions are made by governmental, administrative or judicial authorities, or by families themselves.

- Children must be allowed as active participants in all matters affecting their lives and be free to express their opinions. They have the right to have their views heard and taken seriously.

Source: UNICEF, The Convention on the Rights of the Child

As a direct result of UN initiatives, nearly 90 percent of children in developing countries attend school.

Born: April 8, 1938 in Kumasi, Ghana

Legacy: Revitalizing and reforming the UN as Secretary-General

For more information on Kofi Annan head to: www.un.org/News/ossg/sg/pages/sg_biography.html. Also click on www.un.org/News/ossg/sg/pages/sg_office.html for more information about the role of the Secretary-General.

People in Focus

Beginning his term on January 1, 1997, Kofi Annan became the first Secretary-General to be elected from the United Nations staff. He is also the first person of African descent to hold the position. Shortly after taking office, Annan introduced sweeping reforms that helped the UN adapt to the new era of global affairs. Six months before his five-year term as Secretary-General was to end, Annan was unanimously appointed to serve a second term.

When Annan first took office, the UN was nearly bankrupt and was criticized around the world for its excessive bureaucracy. Annan responded to these problems by cutting staff and budgets, and introducing several management reforms. Faced with a financial shortfall, he also sought closer relations between the UN and the private sector.

Annan first joined the UN in 1962 as an administrative and budget officer with the WHO in Geneva. Since that time, Annan has held a variety of positions within the UN, including High Commissioner for Human Rights and head of the UN Peacekeeping Department from 1993–1995. Annan was head of peacekeeping during a time of unprecedented growth in the size and scope of UN peacekeeping operations. In 1990, after Iraq invaded Kuwait, Annan also facilitated the **repatriation** of more than 900 international staff and the release of western hostages in Iraq. In October 2001, Annan was awarded the Nobel Peace Prize along with the UN.

Annan is well educated. He studied economics in Kumasi; completed undergraduate work in economics at Macalester College in Minnesota; undertook graduate studies in economics in Geneva; and received a Master of Science degree in management from the Massachusetts Institute of Technology. Annan is fluent in English, French, and several African languages.

Map of UN Offices

Figure 1: Principal UN Offices Worldwide

The United States is host to the main decision-making bodies of the UN, which are based in New York and Washington. Most of the other UN headquarters are in Europe. The UN has about 80 information offices across the globe, including 25 in Africa, 16 in Asia and the Pacific, and 12 in Latin America and the Caribbean.

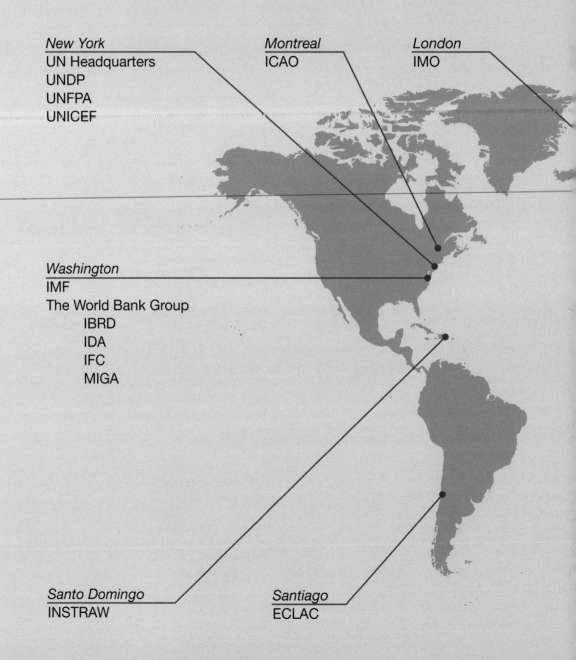

New York
UN Headquarters
UNDP
UNFPA
UNICEF

Montreal
ICAO

London
IMO

Washington
IMF
The World Bank Group
 IBRD
 IDA
 IFC
 MIGA

Santo Domingo
INSTRAW

Santiago
ECLAC

Scale 1:167,000,000

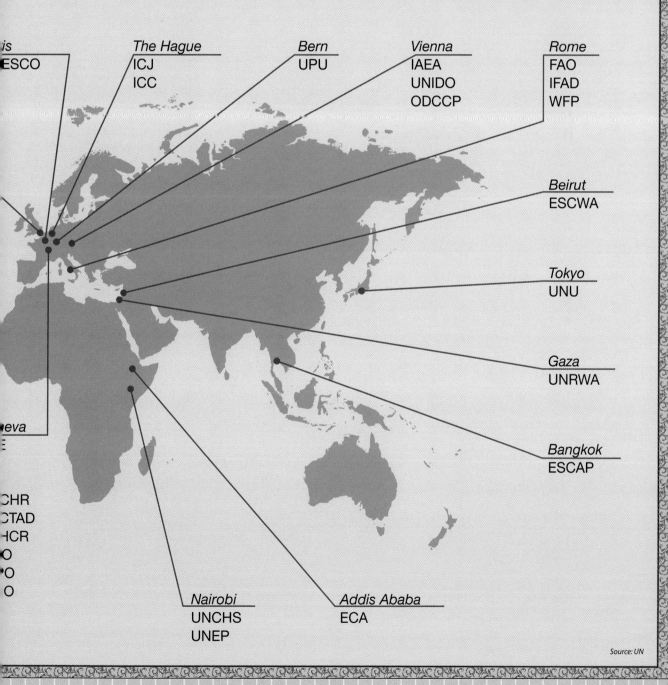

is
ESCO

The Hague
ICJ
ICC

Bern
UPU

Vienna
IAEA
UNIDO
ODCCP

Rome
FAO
IFAD
WFP

Beirut
ESCWA

Tokyo
UNU

Gaza
UNRWA

eva
E

Bangkok
ESCAP

CHR
CTAD
HCR
O
O
O

Nairobi
UNCHS
UNEP

Addis Ababa
ECA

Source: UN

Charting the UN

Figure 2: Who Pays for the UN?
(scale of regular budget assessments 2001, in percent)

Contributions to the UN regular budget are based on the ability of each country to pay. The scale of assessment is reviewed regularly.

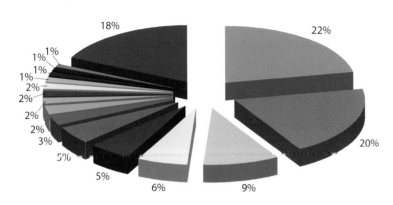

- ☐ U.S.
- ☐ Japan
- ☐ Germany
- ☐ France
- ☐ United Kingdom
- ☐ Italy
- ☐ Canada
- ☐ Spain
- ☐ Brazil
- ☐ Netherlands
- ☐ Australia
- ☐ Korea, Republic of
- ☐ Russia
- ☐ Belgium
- ☐ Sweden
- ☐ Other Countries

Figure 3: The Main Components of the UN System
(showing approximate annual budget in $ million)

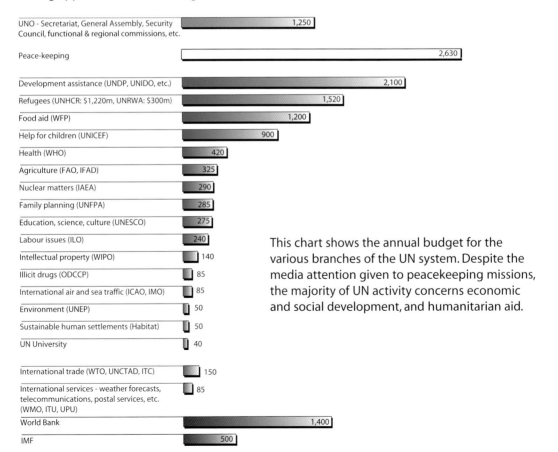

Component	Budget ($ million)
UNO - Secretariat, General Assembly, Security Council, functional & regional commissions, etc.	1,250
Peace-keeping	2,630
Development assistance (UNDP, UNIDO, etc.)	2,100
Refugees (UNHCR: $1,220m, UNRWA: $300m)	1,520
Food aid (WFP)	1,200
Help for children (UNICEF)	900
Health (WHO)	420
Agriculture (FAO, IFAD)	325
Nuclear matters (IAEA)	290
Family planning (UNFPA)	285
Education, science, culture (UNESCO)	275
Labour issues (ILO)	240
Intellectual property (WIPO)	140
Illicit drugs (ODCCP)	85
International air and sea traffic (ICAO, IMO)	85
Environment (UNEP)	50
Sustainable human settlements (Habitat)	50
UN University	40
International trade (WTO, UNCTAD, ITC)	150
International services - weather forecasts, telecommunications, postal services, etc. (WMO, ITU, UPU)	85
World Bank	1,400
IMF	500

This chart shows the annual budget for the various branches of the UN system. Despite the media attention given to peacekeeping missions, the majority of UN activity concerns economic and social development, and humanitarian aid.

Figure 4: UN Peacekeeping Missions

More than 750,000 military, police and civilian personnel from more than 110 countries have served in UN peacekeeping operations since 1948.

Ongoing missions *(July 2001)*		Starting date	Uniformed personnel	Participating countries	Cost 1998-99
UNTSO	(UN Truce Supervision Organisation – Jerusalem)	1948	153	23	$22.8 m
UNMOGIP	(UN Military Observer Group in India & Pakistan)	1949	45	9	$7.3 m
UNFICYP	(UN Peace-keeping Force in Cyprus)	1964	1,246	15	$42.4 m
UNDOF	(UN Disengagement Observer Force – Syrian Golan Heights)	1974	1,130	6	$35.7 m
UNIFIL	(UN Interim Force in Lebanon)	1978	3,652	10	$106.2 m*
UNIKOM	(UN Iraq-Kuwait Observation Mission)	1991	1,095	32	$52.8 m
MINURSO	(UN Mission for the Referendum in Western Sahara)	1991	263	25	$50.5 m
UNOMIG	(UN Observer Mission in Georgia)	1993	106	23	$27.9 m
UNMIBH	(UN Mission in Bosnia and Herzegovina)	1995	1,678	44	$144.7 m
UNMOP	(UN Mission of Observers in Prevlaka – Croatia)	1996	27	24	$2 m
UNMIK	(UN Interim Administration Mission in Kosovo)	1999	n/a	n/a	n/a
UNTAET	(UN Transitional Administration in East Timor)	1999	9,614	30	$563 m
UNAMSIL	(UN Mission in Sierra Leone)	1999	16,664	32	$293.3 m*
MONUC	(UN Organization Mission in the Democratic Republic of the Congo	1999	2,398	42	$209.1 m*
UNMEE	(UN Mission in Ethiopia and Eritrea)	2000	3,870	46	$96 m*

*numbers are for half year only

Other UN-authorised missions *(i.e., delegated to regional forces)*

SFOR	(NATO-led stabilization force in Bosnia)	1996	30,000	over 30	est. $4,000 m
KFOR	(NATO-led protection force in Kosovo)	1999	est. requirement 55,000	20 – 30	est. annual cost $6,000 m
ECOMOG	(Economic Community of West African States Military Observer Group in Liberia, Sierra Leone and Guinea-Bissau – mainly Nigerian and Ghanaian troops)	1991	15,000	n.a.	n.a.

Completed UN peace-keeping missions

UNEF 1	(First UN Emergency Force – Gaza) 1956-67
UNOGIL	(UN Observation Group in Lebanon) 1958
ONUC	(UN Operation in the Congo) 1960-64
UNSF	(UN Security Force in West Iran) 1962-63
UNYOM	(UN Yemen Observation Mission) 1963-64
DOMREP	(Mission of the Secretary-General in the Dominican Republic) 1965-66
UNIPOM	(UN India-Pakistan Observation Mission) 1965-66
UNEF II	(Second UN Emergency Force – Suez Canal and Sinai) 1973-79
UNGOMAP	(UN Good Offices Mission in Afghanistan and Pakistan) 1988-90
UNIIMOG	(UN Iran-Iraq Military Observer Group) 1988-91
UNAVEM I	(UN Angola Verification Mission I) 1989-91
UNTAG	(UN Transition Assistance Group – Angola and Namibia) 1989-90
ONUCA	(UN Observer Group in Central America) 1989-92
UNAVEM II	(UN Angola Verification Mission II) 1991-95
ONUSAL	(UN Observer Mission in El Salvador) 1991-95
UNAMIC	(UN Advance Mission in Cambodia) 1991-92
UNPROFOR	(UN Protection Force – former Yugoslavia) 1992-95
UNTAC	(UN Transitional Authority in Cambodia) 1992-93
UNOSOM I	(UN Operation in Somalia I) 1992-93
ONUMOZ	(UN Operation in Mozambique) 1992-94

UNOSOM II	(UN Operation in Somalia II) 1993-95
UNOMUR	(UN Observer Mission Uganda-Rwanda) 1993-94
UNOMIL	(UN Observer Mission in Liberia) 1993-97
UNMIH	(UN Mission in Haiti) 1993-96
UNAMIR	(UN Assistance Mission for Rwanda) 1993-96
UNASOG	(UN Aouzou Strip Observer Group – Chad) 1994
UNAVEM III	(UN Angola Verification Mission III) 1995-97
UNCRO	(UN Confidence Restoration Operation in Croatia) 1995-96
UNPREDEP	(UN Preventive Deployment Force – Macedonia) 1995-99
UNTAES	(UN Transitional Administration for Eastern Slavonia, Baranja and Western Sirmium – Croatia) 1996-98
UNSMIH	(UN Support Mission in Haiti) 1996-97
MINUGUA	(UN Verification Mission in Guatemala) 1997
MONUA	(UN Observer Mission in Angola) 1997-99
UNTMIH	(UN Transition Mission in Haiti) 1997
UNSPG	(UN Civilian Police Support Group - Croatia) 1998
UNOMSIL	(UN Observer Mission in Sierra Leone) 1998-1999
UNMOT	(UN Mission of Observers in Tajikistan) 1994-2000
MIPONUH	(UN Civilian Police Mission in Haiti) 1997-2000
MINURCA	(UN Mission in the Central African Republic 1998-2000

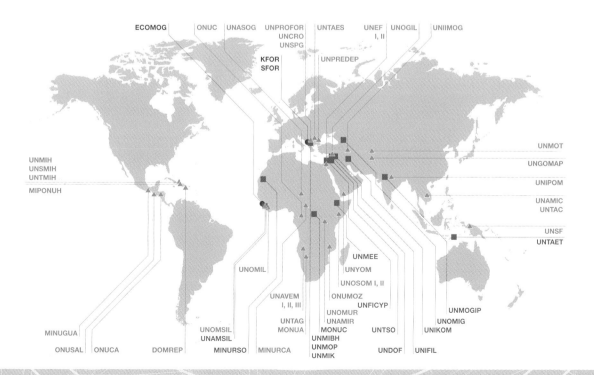

Peace, Law, and Justice

During the Cold War, nobody expected much of the UN. The UN's impact on world events was

In 1988, UN peacekeeping forces were awarded the Nobel Peace Prize for their efforts to build peace and security throughout the world.

quite small. There were relatively few peacekeeping missions, and with about 400 vetoes in the Security Council, the UN was at a standstill. The UN only listened to disagreements between countries or acted as border police when it was in the best interests of the world's most powerful countries. After 1987,

the influence of the last leader of the Soviet Union, Mikhail Gorbachev, changed the tone of the Security Council and introduced a new spirit of cooperation into UN activities.

However, the UN is not a world government. It does not have economic power, nor does it have its own military power. It

THE UN REFUGEE AGENCY

The Office of the UN High Commissioner for Refugees (UNHCR) was established on December 14, 1950, to help people who have been displaced from their homes as a result of natural disasters, persecution, or war. The agency helps refugees by providing basic necessities such as food, shelter, medicine, and water. The UNHCR also works to find homes for refugees, whether it be helping refugees return to their homes, or helping them find new homes in other countries. Since it was established, the UNHCR has helped an estimated 50 million people.

Estimated Number of Refugees Worldwide (January 2001)	
Asia	8,450,000
Africa	6,072,900
Europe	5,571,700
North America	1,047,100
Latin America & Caribbean	575,600
Oceania	76,000
Total	**21,793,300**

depends entirely on the support of its members. Whatever decisions are made in the General Assembly or the Security Council, the United Nations is powerless to act without money. Members have rarely matched their sentiments with cash. Throughout the 1990s and into the 21st century, the United Nations has struggled with inadequate budgets and lack of resources, especially for peacekeeping missions.

The UN may intervene in disagreements between countries, but the UN Charter forbids it to become involved in disagreements between people within the same country, such as in the case of civil war. However, the international community is increasingly turning to the UN whenever there is a conflict or humanitarian crisis anywhere in the world.

> ### The UN is powerless to act without money.

The strength of the UN is the idea of uniting all the world's countries behind the same cause. However, this can also be a weakness. As the UN becomes more involved in disagreements between and within countries, it risks criticism if it is unable to settle those disagreements. Often, the countries that are most critical of the UN are the same ones that have failed to pay their dues to the UN or have failed to support UN military action by providing soldiers or other resources.

Some people would like to see the UN develop into a powerful diplomatic and military tool that acts for the good of the entire world. In the early 1990s, there were signs that such change was taking place. However, a renewed lack of trust between the East and the West has created more disagreement in the Security Council. In the late 1990s, many countries, such as Russia and China, were concerned that the North Atlantic Treaty Organization (NATO) had become an international police force acting on behalf of the UN. There have also been concerns over the UN's new interpretation of international law, which has allowed the UN to interfere in disputes within countries.

The UN faces less criticism when it devotes its energies to social development, humanitarian aid, and general support for human rights— its main role during the first 40 years of its existence. Unable to contribute much to world peace during the Cold War years, the UN devoted its energy to economic development, social justice, and human rights. Though environmental concerns were not addressed in the original UN Charter, "**green**

issues" have also become an important focus of UN activity.

In addition to helping the environment, the UN has funded scientists, engineers, and others to study weather, communication systems, air and sea transportation, and nuclear energy. UN advisors have

---

Environmental concerns have become an important part of the UN's activities.

---

provided more than one billion people with access to safe drinking water and sanitation. They have also helped control many diseases through vaccinations and research.

Unfortunately, the UN has a poor record when it comes to maintaining peace and

improving human development. Despite its original mandate to promote world peace, the world is still burdened with violence. In addition to the current war against terrorism, which is directed primarily against the Taliban in Afghanistan, civil wars are still being fought in many parts of the world. These conflicts have turned millions of people into refugees, as they are forced to leave their homes in search of a safe place to live.

The UN has also made little impact on the standard of living in developing countries. In fact, the gap in living standards between rich and poor countries is more than twice what it was 50 years ago. While the UN still has a long way to go in its quest to solve international political, economic, and social problems, it has managed to accomplish many positive achievements.

KEY CONCEPTS

Civil War A civil war is a conflict between opposing forces within the same country. Civil wars can result from a variety of factors, including land disputes and political, religious, or ethnic differences.

Taliban Islamic fundamentalist movement in Afghanistan, which was created in 1994 by Mullah Mohammed Omar. Although the Taliban had gained control of the vast majority of the country by the late 1990s, most countries in

the world did not recognize it as the legitimate ruling party of Afghanistan. While in power, the Taliban imposed strict rules— women were not allowed to work outside their homes, and men were forced to grow their beards long. After the Taliban refused to hand over Osama bin Laden, who was wanted for the September 11, 2001, terrorist attacks on America, the U.S. began bombing Taliban military positions. The bombings helped anti-Taliban forces to reclaim the country.

NATO The North Atlantic Treaty Organization is an international organization created in 1949 to promote the defense and security of the Western allies during the Cold War.

War crimes War crimes are violations of the laws and customs of war as established in the conventions adopted at The Hague Conferences of 1899 and 1904.

 The International Court of Justice is based in The Hague, the Netherlands.

INTERNATIONAL COURT OF JUSTICE

When countries disagree over landownership, they may agree to take the matter to the International Court of Justice (ICJ). The ICJ makes legal decisions based only upon the principles agreed upon by the world's nations. Unfortunately, fewer than a third of UN countries have accepted the Court's authority. Countries that have accepted the ruling include Egypt, India, Japan, Nigeria, and the United Kingdom. Some countries, such as China, France, Russia, and the U.S., have been unwilling to accept the authority of the ICJ. Other countries will accept the Court's authority on some matters but not on others. The Court has judged more than 75 cases since its creation in 1945.

The International Court of Justice has 15 judges elected for 9-year terms by the General Assembly and the Security Council. Judges are chosen for their qualifications, not their nationality, but no two judges can be citizens of the same country.

The ICJ is not the same as the new International Criminal Court (ICC), which will also be based in The Hague. The ICC will become a permanent court once 60 countries have ratified the Rome Statute of the ICC. The Security Council set up the "International Criminal Tribunal for the former Yugoslavia" in 1993. In November 2001, former Yugoslav President Slobodan Milosevic was charged with **genocide** by the tribunal. This historic case marks the first time a head of state has been charged with genocide under international law. A similar war crimes tribunal for Rwanda was established in 1994.

ACHIEVEMENTS OF THE UN

☐ Since 1945, the UN has helped to negotiate more than 170 peace agreements.

☐ About 50 UN peacekeeping missions were established in the 1990s.

☐ The UN has helped to disarm countries with agreements such as the Nuclear Non-Proliferation Treaty, Nuclear Free Zones, the Land Mines Convention, and the Chemical Weapons Convention.

☐ The UN has helped draw up about 500 **multilateral** agreements.

☐ In 1948, the Universal Declaration of Human Rights provided the foundation for UN conventions on genocide, torture, refugees, racial discrimination, women's rights, the rights of children, and for the global monitoring efforts of the UN High Commissioner for Human Rights.

☐ UN programs have helped increase average life expectancy in the developing world from 37 to 67 years since 1960.

☐ Child immunization against common diseases increased from 5 percent in 1974 to 80 percent in the 1990s.

☐ With the help of the UN, smallpox has been eradicated, and polio should soon follow.

☐ Each year, the UN helps about 50 million displaced or hungry people by providing food, medical aid, and emergency shelter.

☐ The UN has helped to protect the ozone layer (Montreal Protocol); reduce greenhouse gas emissions (Framework Convention on Climate Change, Kyoto Protocol); and preserve the natural environment (UN conventions on **desertification**, biological diversity, and trade in endangered species).

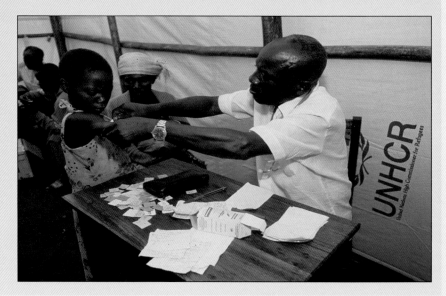

☐ The UN has helped with the safety of international air and sea transportation, the delivery of mail, and the use of radio waves and satellite positioning systems. The UN has also funded technology that allows telephones and computers to communicate with each other.

International Judge

Duties: Settle legal disputes according to international law and provide legal advice to international organizations and agencies

Education: Must be qualified in country of citizenship to be appointed to the highest judicial office, or be a jurist of recognized competence in international law

Interests: Law, justice, and international affairs

Navigate to the UN's International Law Web site: www.un.org/law. Also click on www.icj-cij.org for more information on the International Court of Justice.

Careers in Focus

The International Court of Justice (ICJ) is the main judicial arm of the UN. Located at the Peace Palace in The Hague, the Netherlands, it began its judicial functions in 1946, when it replaced the Permanent Court of International Justice, which had functioned since 1922. The ICJ is made up of 15 judges, who are elected to 9-year terms by the UN General Assembly and Security Council. All 15 judges must be of different nationality and may not come from the same country. The job of the judges is to settle the legal disputes submitted by member countries of the UN according to international law, and to give advice on legal questions referred to it by authorized international organizations and agencies.

An international judge in this court is a very important figure in international affairs. Judges do not represent their governments, but instead are independent magistrates. The judges must possess the qualifications required in their respective countries for appointment to the highest judicial offices, or have recognized competence in international law. Present judges of the ICJ represent a range of countries, from France, China, and Hungary, to Egypt, Sierra Leone, and Madagascar.

Many of the judges had served long, illustrious careers in their own countries before being elected to the ICJ. Many have been professors of law, or have received honorary doctorates. Most of the ICJ judges have degrees in political science or law, and many have doctorates. They have served international organizations and have sat on human rights boards.

The UN's Money Problems

Since the UN was established in 1945, there have been about 150 wars. More than 20 million people have died in those wars. Newspapers and television screens are filled with stories of **atrocities** that are committed across the world. Human rights abuses persist. The problems with the environment continue. Governments put the interests of their own countries before the good of the whole world. Terrorism, ethnic cleansing, torture, the massacre of women

Many Secretaries-General have complained that the UN does not have a predictable source of funding.

and children—the list of brutalities is long.

To put an end to these atrocities, the UN needs to become more involved. But the UN cannot operate without the cooperation of the most powerful countries in the world. The UN also cannot operate without money. If member states continue to withhold their dues, the UN will be forced to shut down.

Many Secretaries-General have complained that the UN does not have a predictable source of funding. During the 1990s, the UN had unpaid peacekeeping bills of $1 billion to $3 billion per year. Many nongovernmental agencies have been generous by giving money to the UN. Time Warner owner

As the number of refugees rose dramatically in the 1990s, the UNHCR's annual budget doubled to more than $1 billion.

Ted Turner even gave a personal gift of $1 billion to the UN in 1997. While these gifts have helped with emergency relief, human rights, and education, only governments are allowed to finance peacekeeping operations.

The failure of member states to pay their assessed contributions on time is a constant headache. What makes the situation worse is that the world's richest country, the United States, is the biggest offender. In the 1990s, U.S. **arrears** were typically between $1 billion and $2 billion. This is a high proportion of the UN's operating budget. Former Soviet Union countries, such as the Ukraine, are in arrears because of economic problems. There are many other countries which do not pay their dues, though the poorest of them only have to pay the minimum contribution— 0.001 percent of the total UN budget. When member nations, such as the United States, fail to pay their dues to the UN, the UN missions throughout the world cannot be fulfilled. Human and environmental crises require the world's immediate attention and the resources of the UN.

Member nations are also obligated to provide military forces to support the resolutions of the Security Council. In practice, the UN has a difficult time getting member states to honor these commitments. In 1994, the Secretary-General told the Security Council that 35,000 troops would be needed

Since 1948, the United Nations has spent nearly $24 billion on peacekeeping operations.

RUNNING OUT OF MONEY

The UN has severe cash-flow problems. Unlike the World Bank, it is not allowed to borrow money in international **capital markets** to finance its operations. The UN depends entirely on money from its members. During the mid-1990s, the UN was forced to borrow money from peacekeeping funds in order to pay day-to-day activities in other core areas. A smaller peacekeeping budget has squeezed UN cash flow more tightly than ever.

to maintain "safe areas" in Bosnia. However, member states authorized only 7,500 troops. It then took an entire year before the troops were finally called into action. Without adequate support, many "safe areas" fell to Serbian forces, resulting in the deaths of thousands of civilians. Member states also failed to take quick military action to prevent the widely predicted genocide that took place in Rwanda in 1994.

The failure of UN member countries to provide money and military resources for **preventive** missions is very expensive in the long term. Preventive action often costs much less than more involved peacekeeping missions. War in

At various times in 1999, more than 4,000 Kosovar refugees crossed the Macedonian border every hour to escape the threat of ethnic cleansing.

the Balkans has already cost more than all other United Nations peacekeeping missions combined.

KEY CONCEPTS

Ethnic cleansing The systematic removal of people from a region is referred to as ethnic cleansing. The victims are targeted based on their ethnicity or religious background, and the removal can take the form of either genocide or forced expulsion.

NGOs NGOs, also known as nongovernmental organizations,

do not belong to any political party and are not affiliated with any government body. These non-profit organizations are typically run by volunteers. NGOs often represent special interests, such as the environment or human rights. Increasingly, the UN is cooperating with NGOs in its efforts to create a civil society for all. More than 1,500 NGOs

cooperate with the UN, sharing information.

Globalization During the latter half of the 20th century, new information and communication technologies, such as the Internet, combined with new trends in international commerce to produce an interconnected world.

DOES THE WORLD NEED A BANK?

PROS	CONS
Founded during World War II, the World Bank initially helped rebuild Europe after the war. Its first loan was to France in 1947 for post-war **reconstruction**—a sum of $250 million. The World Bank is now 183 member-countries strong. Its mandate is to give aid to **transition economies** that require **rehabilitation**, and to reduce global poverty.	In April 2000, between 3,000 and 5,000 protesters marched from the White House to the World Bank's Washington, D.C. headquarters, chanting slogans such as "Defund the Fund," "Break the Bank," and "Dump the Debt." They were protesting what they considered to be the injustices of globalization trends. Below are just a few anti-globalization sentiments.
Since 1963, when it began its education-funding programs, the World Bank has provided over $30 billion in loans and credits. It currently finances 164 projects in 82 countries. In Pakistan, the World Bank leads the initiatives to educate Afghan refugees.	Organizations such as the World Bank and the International Monetary Fund (IMF) do not represent a global community. Instead, they are a select group of central bankers and finance ministers who make decisions without the input of those people that are affected.
As a co-sponsor of UNAIDS, the World Bank has committed more than $1.7 billion to combating the spread of HIV/AIDS around the world, and has pledged that "no country with an effective HIV/AIDS-fighting strategy in place will go without funding."	Voting power in these organizations is based on a one dollar/one vote structure. This means that the seven richest countries in the world hold almost 50 percent of the voting power.
As the world's largest external funder of health programs, the World Bank provides the world's poorest nations with basic health and nutrition, in hopes of reducing poverty and promoting economic growth.	Wealthy countries often benefit at the expense of the poor. In order to receive debt relief, countries are forced to adopt practices determined by the World Bank, such as allowing foreign investment, **privatization**, and decreased social spending.
The World Bank commits about $1.3 billion in new lending each year for health, nutrition, and population projects in the developing world.	About 80 percent of malnourished children worldwide live in countries where World Bank/IMF policies encourage local farmers to shift from producing food for their families to producing **cash crops** for export.
The World Bank strongly supports debt relief, linking with the IMF to create the Heavily Indebted Poor Countries Initiative (HIPC). Today, 23 countries are receiving debt relief, amounting to $34 billion.	The shift toward export-based economies has also meant that many developing countries are exploiting their natural resources, often resulting in environmental devastation.

NATO and the UN Army

If one country invades another, the UN can call upon its members to provide an army to deal with the situation. This is what happened in Kuwait during the Gulf War of 1990–1991. However, if fighting breaks out within a country,

▓▓ **Canada and the island nation of Fiji are the only countries to have participated in nearly every peacekeeping mission since 1948.**

the UN has no power under its Charter to intervene, unless the UN is invited to do so by the country concerned.

Under Chapter VIII of the UN Charter, the Security Council may use regional agencies, such as NATO, for military action. The peacekeeping mission in Kosovo, Yugoslavia, was authorized by the Security Council in June 1999. However, the bombing of

Kosovo by NATO started before June 1999, and was done without a Security Council vote. NATO knew that China and Russia would not have permitted NATO to bomb Kosovo if they voted on the action before it started. Western leaders argued that military action could be justified on humanitarian grounds. Prior to the NATO bombing campaign, Albanians in Kosovo had been the victims of ethnic

cleansing. NATO believed that without outside intervention more innocent people in Kosovo would be killed, injured, tortured, or displaced.

NATO's decision to intervene in Kosovo marked a major change in the way Western countries dealt with atrocities carried out within a country's borders. This change in attitude hints at a future where the affairs of any given country may be subject to the judgment and interference of outside forces, such as NATO. While few will argue against the prevention of atrocities, such as ethnic cleansing, many people are nervous about who is given the power to decide when and where to intervene. Some people are concerned that NATO has become an international police force, resorting to violence when it sees fit, without the prior approval of the international community. By comparison, the war on terrorism, though not a UN action, had the prior approval of the UN.

Some critics think that the UN only involves itself in disputes that interest the United

---

The UN now has a "standby system" of more than 100,000 soldiers from 80 different countries.

States or Europe. Critics point to the UN's support of the current war on terrorism and NATO's actions in Kosovo as proof. After all, the UN and NATO have put 80,000 troops into the Balkans and have kept more than 6,000 peacekeepers in the Middle East for decades. At the same time, the UN has been less involved with the problems in Africa, where the violence has been as great or greater, but where the United States does not have any interest.

The UN army that was planned under the UN Charter in 1945 was never formed. However, there is now a "standby system" of more than 100,000 soldiers from 80 different countries. A UN "high-readiness" brigade has been established, with headquarters in Copenhagen, Denmark. There are signs that the UN may obtain some serious independent military backing at last—though on terms set by the major powers. But even when countries promise soldiers and equipment, they are often slow to send them into the field. Another problem is that international forces sometimes

PEACEKEEPING IN THE MIDDLE EAST

One of the UN's longest-running peacekeeping missions has been UN Interim Force in Lebanon (UNIFIL). This mission has been ongoing since 1978, when Israel invaded southern Lebanon. In response, the Palestinian Liberation Organization, based in refugee camps in the area, attacked Israel in small guerilla campaigns. The Security Council called for an end to Israel's military action and the withdrawal of forces.

Israel's controversial policies in the Middle East explain why it is the only UN member that has never served on the Security Council.

UNIFIL QUICK FACTS

Headquarters: Naqoura, Lebanon

Troops: 4,486

Support Staff: 471

Fatalities: 244

Budget 2001: $106.2 million

Military Contributors: Fiji, Finland, France, Ghana, India, Ireland, Italy, Poland, and Ukraine

A TROUBLED PEACEMAKER

The UN's credibility as a peacemaker was gravely weakened in the 1990s by its inability to restrain the warring parties in the Balkans, where large-scale atrocities were carried out after the breakup of former Yugoslavia. The memory of such humiliations helped stiffen the resolve of NATO when the ethnic cleansing of Kosovo began to escalate in late 1998. Though many experts had been forecasting a conflict in Kosovo since it lost its **autonomy** in 1989, the Security Council took little preventive action. The only preventive deployment of troops in UN history was the UN Preventive Deployment Force—Macedonia (UNPREDEP) in Macedonia between 1995 and 1999. Continuation of this mission was vetoed by China in early 1999.

The UN's original role in world affairs is one of peacekeeper. However, the UN is increasingly forced to resort to or support violence as a means of preventing further violence. This new role contradicts the UN's other role as a provider of humanitarian aid.

The UN is sometimes tempted to let regional organizations such as NATO handle the military side of its role as peacekeeper. For such a solution to be acceptable, a proper legal basis is essential—and that means getting authority from a Security Council that more truly reflects the current global community.

UN humanitarian missions can no longer depend on safe passage. This UN convoy, en route to the Balkans to help refugees, stopped so that staff could put on flak jackets to protect themselves from snipers.

do not know which general to follow. The generals often disagree on strategies and authority. This was a problem in Bosnia until NATO stepped in.

Prior to the campaign in the Balkans, the biggest UN operation was in Cambodia in 1992–1993, where it established an interim government. Most UN missions have been much less ambitious. They often focus on monitoring cease-fires or overseeing elections. There were only 13 UN peacekeeping missions between 1945 and 1988. Since then, there have been about 40 more. Unfortunately, there is no shortage of disagreements in the world.

KEY CONCEPTS

Interim government Interim governments manage the affairs of a country during periods of transition until a formal government can be established through an election or other process. In 1999, the UN established an interim government in Kosovo under the direct leadership of the UN.

Duties: Monitor cease-fires, supervise elections, and provide humanitarian aid
Education: High School
Interests: Helping others and maintaining peace

Navigate to the UN's Peacekeeping Web site: www.un.org/Depts/dpko/dpko/home_bottom.htm for more information on peacekeeping. Also click on www.un.org/Depts/dpko/field for information on field employment with peacekeeping operations.

Careers in Focus

UN peacekeepers—or "blue helmets," as they are often called—can perform a variety of tasks, but must always play a neutral role. They are sent into areas of conflict to ensure agreements made between opposing sides are being followed. UN peacekeepers are sometimes placed in the middle of a battle. They stand between two warring parties, negotiating with military officers on either side, providing a channel of communication.

A peacekeeper must have a variety of skills. He or she must be brave, be in excellent physical condition, have a genuine desire to help people, and be willing to travel the world. Communication skills are also very important, as peacekeepers rely on words, not weapons, to maintain peace. Those who are fluent in more than one language or who have experience working in developing countries have an advantage. In addition, a peacekeeper must be willing to work in difficult and dangerous conditions, and must be available for duty on short notice. Since peacekeeping forces are drawn from the armed forces of UN member countries, they must meet the qualifications established by their nation's army.

Peacekeepers must be willing to take risks and endanger their own lives to preserve the lives of others. More than 1,600 peacekeepers have been killed on UN missions. Peacekeepers are only lightly armed. The forces travel in armored vehicles and carry automatic rifles, but they do not have artillery, tanks, or other heavy weapons. Peacekeepers are often caught in the middle when cease-fires break down. They can be deliberately attacked, especially if one of the warring sides doubts their neutrality. Peacekeepers cannot use their weapons except in self-defense.

The UN in the 21st Century

The war against terrorism and the peacekeeping activities of the UN are well covered by the media. However, less coverage is devoted to the remaining 80 percent of United Nations efforts, such as economic and social development, humanitarian aid, and improvements in human rights.

Despite terrorist threats, the world is a safer, healthier, and friendlier place than it would be without the UN. The UN has set international standards for human rights. Much effort goes into support for good governance, civil law and order, equal rights for women, and democratic elections. The UN also helps poor countries build health and education services. From mine clearance to emergency food aid, the United Nations is a force for good and deserves maximum support from governments and the public.

Many developing countries believe that UN agencies have done more to help rich countries than poorer countries. Farming experts from the **developed world**, for example, have helped to spread the use of

▨ **With more than 3.6 million displaced people, Afghanistan has the largest refugee population in the world.**

fertilizers, chemicals, and intensive farming techniques around the world. But the poor countries that receive this assistance complain that the large farming businesses helping them are making money by doing so. Help from the World Bank and the International Monetary Fund (IMF) often comes at the price of compliance with the world's richest nations.

MILLENNIUM SUMMIT

In September 2000, New York hosted the largest-ever gathering of world leaders at the UN's Millennium Summit. The three-day summit was attended by 150 heads of state or government, and 191 nations in total. The meeting examined international issues and explored the UN's role in dealing with those issues. Each head of state could speak for five minutes.

The main message to emerge from the summit was a need to make globalization work for all countries, not just the developed world. Many individuals in the developed world have benefited from the new opportunities globalization has afforded. However, for many people in the world, globalization is considered a threat to their way of life.

"As obstacles of distance shrink, and barriers of time disappear, our planet is suddenly a much smaller place. Our lives are being affected by events taking place halfway around the world. Insularity is less and less of an option. No individual, and no country, exists in isolation. All of us live simultaneously in our own communities and in the world at large. This interdependence—of people and products, information and ideas—means that more and more of the challenges we face can no longer be addressed at the national level alone. More and more, the playing field is international."

—*Deputy Secretary-General Louise Fréchette*

SUMMIT QUICK FACTS
Attendance: 150 heads of state
Transportation: 1,300 limousines
Security: 6,000 policemen
Cost of Security and Traffic Control: $10 million

The United Nations does not want to exploit the developing world. Unfortunately, current economic systems tend to benefit whomever has the most money—on a global level, that is the United States, the countries of the European Union, and Japan. People living in "high-income" countries receive more than 70 times the average income of those in "low-income" countries.

Since poverty is a key reason for conflict, the UN's primary goal of international peace and security cannot be achieved without reducing poverty. To this end, the UN has declared the decade 1997–2006 as the International Decade for the Eradication of Poverty. Kofi Annan has called for a closer partnership with business to strengthen the UN's ability to bring about change. While no magic wand can make all of humanity rich, equality and justice are badly needed if peace is to prevail.

BUILDING A GLOBAL CIVIL SOCIETY

The support of NGOs and the general public, linked through the Internet, has become an increasingly important aspect of UN activity. NGOs such as Greenpeace and the International Chamber of Commerce are looking to protect the interests of all humanity and the whole planet. In recent years, pressure from environmentalists and ordinary people has led to the ban on land mines, the creation of a war crimes court, and environmental reform.

The UN is leading an international effort to eradicate land mines, which kill or injure thousands of people each year.

THE GREENING OF THE UN

The UN Charter in 1945 made no reference to the environment. "Green issues" have become increasingly important with each passing decade. The first Earth Summit led to the founding of the UN Environment Programme (UNEP). It took place in Stockholm in 1972. It was followed by the much larger Rio Summit of 1992. The UN has added environmental protection to its list of global issues. Today, the UN tackles environmental problems such as climate change, deforestation, and overfishing.

▨ The UN devotes nearly 80 percent of its efforts to providing developing nations with the tools they require to improve their quality of life, such as access to clean drinking water. Currently, about 2.5 million people die annually from drinking unsafe water.

KEY CONCEPTS

Civil society A society in which economics, cultural activities, and political interaction are organized by private or voluntary arrangements between individuals and groups not directly controlled by the state.

De-mining Before a minefield can be cleared, it must be surveyed, mapped, and marked. Once a minefield has been marked, clearance operations can begin and may make use of three methods. For manual clearance, trained de-miners use metal detectors and long thin prodders to locate the mines. Once the mines are detected, they are destroyed by a controlled explosion. Another option is the use of mine detection dogs, trained to smell explosives underground. Finally, machinery such as armored bulldozers can be used to destroy mines. The UN's Mine Action Programme for Afghanistan (MAPA), which is the world's oldest and largest mine program, has cleared 1.4 million mines in Afghanistan alone.

Time Line of Events

January 18, 1918
American President Woodrow Wilson delivers his speech on the Fourteen Points for peace. The 14th point calls for "a general association of nations" to protect world peace.

November 15, 1920
The first meeting of the League of Nations is held in Geneva. Forty-two nations are represented.

1933
Germany and Japan withdraw from the League of Nations.

October 1943
The Soviet Union, the United Kingdom, the United States, and China say they want a new organization to maintain peace and security.

October 24, 1945
The UN Charter is agreed to by the five permanent members of the Security Council and a majority of other nations. So begins the UN.

January 10, 1946
The first session of the General Assembly meets in London, England.

January 17, 1946
The Security Council meets for the first time in London.

January 24, 1946
The General Assembly adopts its first resolution. It involves a search for peaceful uses of atomic energy and the elimination of atomic and other weapons of mass destruction.

April 1946
The League of Nations officially dissolves.

December 10, 1948
The General Assembly adopts the Universal Declaration of Human Rights.

1949
John Boyd Orr is awarded the Nobel Peace Prize for his work with the FAO.

June 27, 1950
The Security Council approves sending UN troops to protect southern Korea from a northern invasion.

1950
Ralph Bunche wins the Nobel Peace Prize for his work in the Middle East.

1952
The UN finishes the construction of its headquarters in New York. John D. Rockefeller donated the $8.5 million needed to purchase the land.

July 27, 1953
An agreement to end the Korean War is signed between the UN and North Korea.

1954
The UNHCR is awarded the Nobel Peace Prize for helping European refugees after World War II.

November 1956
The first UN peacekeeping force is created to deal with a crisis involving the Suez Canal.

September 18, 1961
Secretary-General Dag Hammarskjöld dies in a plane crash while on a mission to Congo.

Since 1948, the UN has been involved in 54 peacekeeping operations around the world.

1961

Dag Hammarskjöld is awarded the Nobel Peace Prize posthumously.

January 1965

Indonesia withdraws from the UN. It resumes its membership the following year.

1965

UNICEF, the UN Children's Fund, is awarded the 1965 Nobel Peace Prize.

1981

The UNHCR receives its second Nobel Peace Prize, this time for its work in Asia and Africa.

1988

UN peacekeeping operations are awarded the Nobel Peace Prize.

September 2, 1990

The Convention on the Rights of the Child begins.

June 23, 1994

South Africa returns to the General Assembly after a 24-year absence.

November 2000

The Federal Republic of Yugoslavia is admitted as a member of the UN.

September 12, 2001

The General Assembly condemns terrorism, and calls for "international cooperation to prevent and eradicate acts of terrorism."

October 12, 2001

Kofi Annan and the UN share the Nobel Peace Prize.

Concept Web

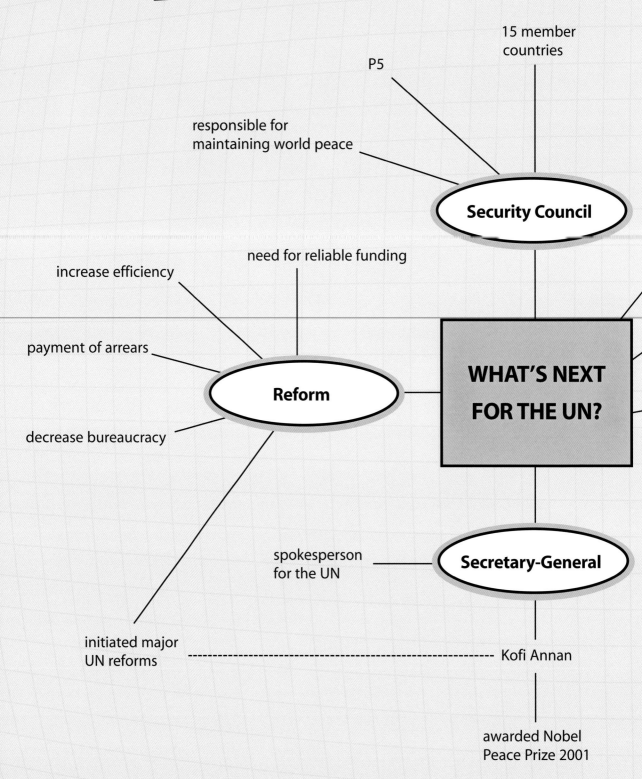

15 member countries

P5

responsible for maintaining world peace

Security Council

need for reliable funding

increase efficiency

payment of arrears

Reform

decrease bureaucracy

WHAT'S NEXT FOR THE UN?

spokesperson for the UN

Secretary-General

initiated major UN reforms

Kofi Annan

awarded Nobel Peace Prize 2001

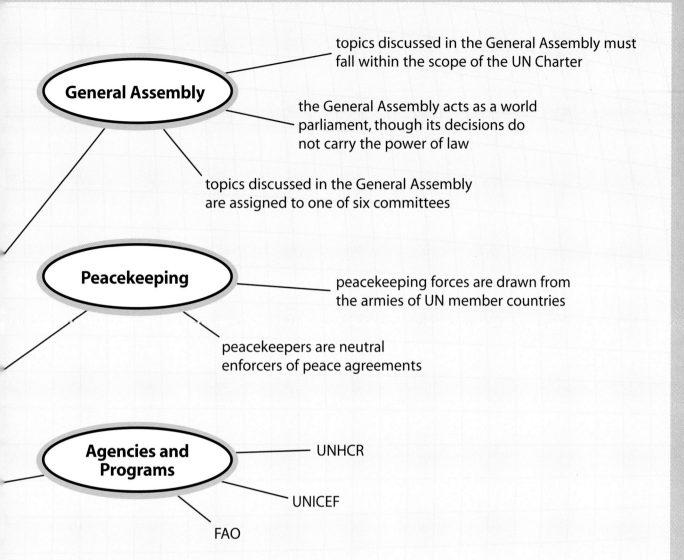

General Assembly
- topics discussed in the General Assembly must fall within the scope of the UN Charter
- the General Assembly acts as a world parliament, though its decisions do not carry the power of law
- topics discussed in the General Assembly are assigned to one of six committees

Peacekeeping
- peacekeeping forces are drawn from the armies of UN member countries
- peacekeepers are neutral enforcers of peace agreements

Agencies and Programs
- UNHCR
- UNICEF
- FAO

MAKE YOUR OWN CONCEPT WEB

A concept web is a useful summary tool. It can also be used to plan your research or help you write an essay or report. To make your own concept web, follow the steps below:

- You will need a large piece of unlined paper and a pencil.
- First, read through your source material, such as *What's Next for the UN?* in the Understanding Global Issues series.
- Write the main idea, or concept, in large letters in the center of the page.
- On a sheet of lined paper, jot down all words, phrases, or lists that you know are connected with the concept. Try to do this from memory.
- Look at your list. Can you group your words and phrases in certain topics or themes? Connect the different topics with lines to the center, or to other "branches."
- Critique your concept web. Ask questions about the material on your concept web:
  Does it all make sense? Are all the links shown? Could there be other ways of looking at it? Is anything missing?
- What more do you need to find out? Develop questions for those areas you are still unsure about or where information is missing. Use these questions as a basis for further research.

Quiz

Multiple Choice

1. The League of Nations was established to:
   a) standardize world currency
   b) create and maintain world peace
   c) protect the environment
   d) all of the above

2. The agenda for UN operations is directed by:
   a) The General Assembly
   b) The League of Nations
   c) The Security Council
   d) all of the above

3. How many countries are permanent members of the Security Council?
   a) four
   b) five
   c) six
   d) fifteen

4. In which year was the UN established?
   a) 1940
   b) 1965
   c) 1905
   d) 1945

5. The International Court of Justice, based in the The Hague, the Netherlands, is responsible for:
   a) solving disputes between countries over landownership
   b) solving trading disputes between countries
   c) prosecution of war crimes, crimes of genocide, and crimes against humanity
   d) all of the above

6. The UN may send an army to deal with internal war within a country:
   a) always
   b) never
   c) only when invited to do so by the country concerned
   d) only when the country concerned is a member of the UN

7. What city is the site of the headquarters of the World Health Organization, the UN High Commissioner for Refugees, and the Economic Commission for Europe?
   a) Paris, France
   b) London, England
   c) Ottawa, Canada
   d) Geneva, Switzerland

Where Did It Happen?

1. The establishment of a war crimes tribunal in 1994.
2. The site of one of the UN's longest-running peacekeeping missions, which began in 1978.
3. The headquarters of the UN's "high-readiness" brigade.
4. The first meeting of the General Assembly in 1946.

True or False

1. During the Cold War, the Security Council worked together to enforce the UN's resolutions.
2. The General Assembly has had to expel a country from the UN for grave misbehavior.
3. Economic sanctions placed on Iraq between 1991 and 1996 are estimated to have resulted in the deaths of more than 500,000 children from lack of medical care and starvation.
4. The UN has been involved in 54 peacekeeping missions.

Answers on page 53

Internet Resources

The following provide more information on the UN and its agencies:

UN
http://www.un.org

The UN Web site provides information and resources that cover the issues, goals, history, and structure of this giant organization. The information on the UN's Web site is available in six different languages. Individuals can search the archive for news articles and reports, maps, and landmark documents. There is a search engine to find topics of interest, as well as FAQs.

UNICEF
http://www.unicef.org

The UNICEF Web site is filled with information about the plight of children across the globe. It contains resources such as statistics, publications, and learning tools. For younger visitors, the Web site even offers games, exhibits, and a free screen saver. Individuals can take part in on-line discussion by clicking on the "Voices of Youth" link.

Some Web sites stay current longer than others. To find other UN Web sites, enter terms such as "United Nations," "peacekeeping," or "General Assembly" into a search engine.

Further Reading

Gorman, Robert F. *Great Debates at the United Nations: An Encyclopedia of Fifty Key Issues, 1945–2000*. Westport, Connecticut: Greenwood Publishing Group, 2001.

Meisler, Stanley. *United Nations: The First Fifty Years*. New York: Atlantic Monthly Press, 1997.

Otunnu, Olara A. (Ed.) *Peacemaking and Peacekeeping for the New Century*. Lanham, Maryland: Rowman & Littlefield Publishing, 1998.

Reinicke, Wolfgang H. (Ed.) *Critical Choices: The United Nations, Networks, and the Future of Global Governance*. Ottawa: IDRC, 2000.

Rikhye, Major General Indar. *The Politics and Practice of United Nations Peacekeeping: Past, Present, and Future*. Cornwallis Park, Nova Scotia: Canadian Peacekeeping Press, 2000.

Taylor, P. J. (Ed.) *World Government*. New York: Oxford University Press, 1990.

Williams, Ian. *The U.N. for Beginners*. New York: Writers and Readers Publishing, 1995.

Answers

Multiple Choice
1. b) 2. a) 3. b) 4. d) 5. a) 6. c) 7. d)

Where Did It Happen?
1. Rwanda 2. Lebanon 3. Copenhagen, Denmark 4. London, England

True or False
1. F 2. F 3. T 4. T

Glossary

arms race: the competition between countries for superiority in the number of weapons held, and in the power of those weapons

arrears: money due that has not been paid

atrocities: very cruel or brutal acts

autonomy: right to self-government

capital markets: financial markets involving institutions that deal with bonds and stocks

cash crops: crops that are considered easy to sell, such as bananas

cease-fires: formal cessations of combat between opposing armed forces

cognitive: relating to the mental processes of perception, memory, judgment, and reasoning

commissions: government agencies with particular purposes

desertification: deterioration of arid land into desert, caused by a change in climate or by overuse by people and/or animals

developed world: those countries that have undergone the process of industrialization

developing countries: those countries that are undergoing the process of industrialization, sometimes collectively referred to as the Third World

dues: fees owed or paid to an organization by members

genocide: systematic measures for the extermination of a national, cultural, religious, or racial group

green issues: environmental concerns

multilateral: involving two or more nations

preventive: devised to stop something from happening

privatization: transferring public property and services from public or government control to private control

ratified: the validation of a formally approved and usually negotiated agreement

reconstruction: the act of rebuilding

reforms: changes made to improve conditions

rehabilitation: act or process of restoring to good condition

repatriation: the returning of a person to his or her own country

rhetoric: language designed to persuade or impress

suppression: forcefully restrained or held back

transition economies: economies that are in the process of changing from one type of economy to another

Index

Photo Credits

Cover: The General Assembly at its 48th Session. (UN/DPI Photo/183790/**E. Kanalstein**); **Title Page**: Crispin Hughs/**Panos Pictures**; **CORBIS/MAGMA**: pages 17, 33 (Reuters New Media Inc.); **Corel**: pages 28, 35, 38, 41; **DigitalVision**: page 45; **Eyewire Inc**: page 13; **National Archives of Canada**: page 6 (CZ0074); **Panos Pictures**: pages 40, 47 (Chris Stowers); **UNHCR**: pages 7, 29, 32b, 34, 36; **UN PHOTOS**: pages 2/3 (UN/DPI Photo/145618/**J. Issac**), 4 (UN/DPI Photo/185518/**A. Brizzi**), 9 (UN/DPI Photo/152408/**L. Gubb**), 10 (UN/DPI Photo/183790/**E. Kanalstein**), 15 (UN/DPI Photo/189133/**E. Schneider**), 18 (UN/DPI Photo/18740/**P. Sudhakaran**), 22 (UN/DPI Photo/152390/**John Issac**), 23 (UN/DPI Photo/193355/**Milton Grant**), 31 (UN/DPI Photo/186850/**A. Brizzi**), 32t (UN/DPI Photo/187532/**Eskinder Debebe**), 42 (UN/DPI Photo/153554/**J. Isaac**), 44 (UN/DPI Photo/157921/**J. Isaac**).